BEETLES

Contents

Original title of the book in Spanish: El Fascinante Mundo de...
Los Escarabajos.
© Copyright Parramón Ediciones, S.A.
Published by Parramón Ediciones, S.A.,
Barcelona, Spain

Author: Maria Ángels Julivert
Illustrator: Marcel Socías Studios

English text © Copyright 1995 by Barron's Educational Series, Inc.

All inquiries should be addressed to:
Barron's Educational Series, Inc.
250 Wireless Boulevard
Hauppauge, New York 11788
Library of Congress Catalog Card No. 95-7404
International Standard Book No. 0-8120-9423-9

Library of Congress Cataloging-in-Publication Data
Julivert, Maria Ángels,
    [Escarabajos. English]
    The fascinating world of—beetles / by Maria Ángels Julivert;
    illustrations by Marcel Socías Studios.—1st ed.
        p.   cm.
    Includes index.
    ISBN 0-8120-9423-9
    1. Beetles—Juvenile literature.   [1. Beetles.]   I. Marcel
Socías Studios.   II. Title.
QL576.2.J8513   1995   95-7404
595.76—dc20   CIP
                                                     AC

Printed in Spain
5678   9960   987654321

THE FASCINATING WORLD OF...

BEETLES

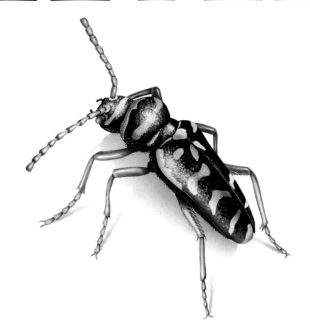

by

Maria Ángels Julivert

Illustrations by Marcel Socías Studios

BARRON'S

NUMEROUS AND COLORFUL

Beetles belong to the order of **Coleoptera,** which consists of a large number of families.They are, without a doubt, the most numerous group of insects. There are more than 300,000 known species and the numbers increase each year with new discoveries.

These animals have colonized all environments except the sea. They live in forests, woods, fields, towns, plains, inhospitable deserts, and so on. Some are even aquatic and live in lakes, ponds, and reservoirs. Some inhabit trees, others live on leaves, and some in dark caves. Finally, some exist as **parasites** of other animals.

Many **Coleoptera** are dark in color, but there are also some that are very colorful: their **elytra** (the front pair of wings) can have metallic shades, with beautiful colors or strange shapes. In beetles the most frequent colors are greens, reds, yellows, and blacks, and often these colors combine to create striking contrasts.

Right: A cerambycid or long-horned, wood-boring beetle with long antennae, climbing up a tree; a ladybug in flight, a poplar leaf-beetle, and a chrysomela.

Below: From their different outlines, one can see the diversity of their forms.

Left: The goliath beetle lives in tropical Africa.

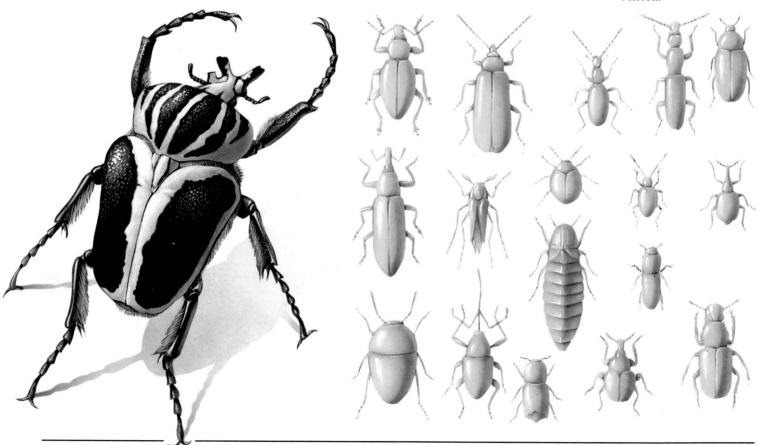

A PROTECTIVE CASE

Beetles are insects, like bees, flies, grasshoppers, dragonflies, and butterflies.

Their bodies are divided into three parts: head, thorax, and abdomen. On the head are located the mouth parts and the sense organs: two complex eyes and a pair of antennae.

On the thorax, which is made up of **segments**, they have two pairs of wings and six legs. The legs consist of various parts or **articles**, which are linked to each other and end in a pair of claws. The feet of some beetles have been modified to enable them to swim, run, dig, and more.

The front pair of a beetle's wings, or **elytra**, are very hard and protect the second pair, which are fine and made of membrane to allow them to fly. Although the hind wings are longer, in their resting position they are entirely covered by the **elytra**.

In most insects, the **elytra** cover the whole abdomen, although in some species they are very short. Their shape and form vary. They can be smooth, rough, marked, furrowed, or grooved.

Almost all beetles can fly, and only a few species have lost their hind wings or have fused **elytra**, but they are exceptions.

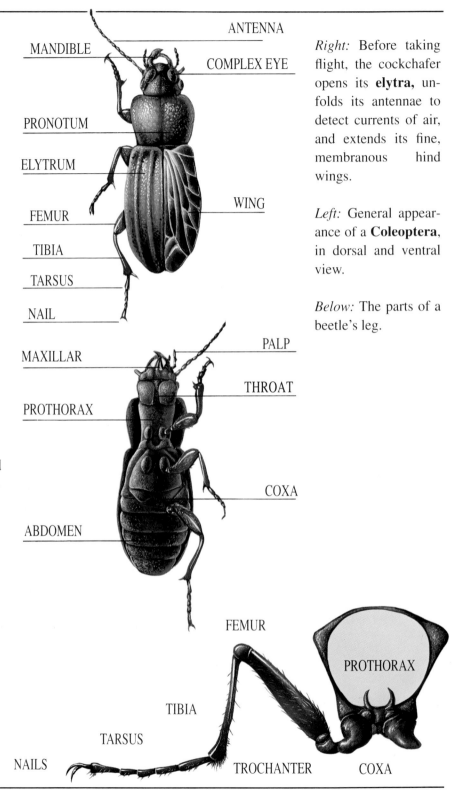

Right: Before taking flight, the cockchafer opens its **elytra,** unfolds its antennae to detect currents of air, and extends its fine, membranous hind wings.

Left: General appearance of a **Coleoptera**, in dorsal and ventral view.

Below: The parts of a beetle's leg.

ANTENNAE AND LEGS FOR SMELLING

Beetles' main sense organs are situated on the head, although they have many sensory hairs in different parts of the body, for example on the legs.

Sight and smell are the most well-developed senses, and it is with these that insects can recognize one another, locate food, and detect danger.

Adult beetles, with the exception of some species that are blind, have a pair of complex eyes, made up of numerous surfaces: the **ocelli**. The larvae, in common with some adults, have various simple eyes, called **ommatidia**.

They can detect smells using their antennae, which have numerous sensory receptors, but they also have olfactory hairs on their legs and in their **palps**. For some species smell is essential because it allows them to locate their food and to find a mate. The necrophagous beetles detect the bodies of animals by their smell, even over long distances.

A variable number of sections, called **articles**, form the antennae.

The size and shape of these varies greatly from one species to another, and even between the male and the female of the same species. They can be longer than the beetle's body, short, serrated, or end in a hammer shape. They clean them frequently using their palps and their legs.

Beetles do not hear in the same way that we do, but instead they detect vibrations by means of sensory hairs located in different parts of the body.

Right: A long-horned or wood-boring beetle (cerambycid) with long antennae in the form of a chain and a cellar beetle with short antennae, which lives in storerooms and basements.

Above: Detail of the head, showing the complex eyes, the antennae, the **palps**, and the forelegs.

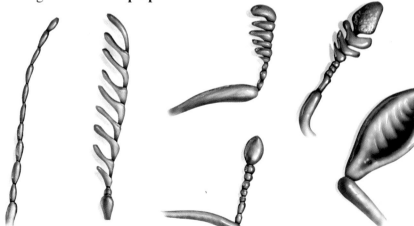

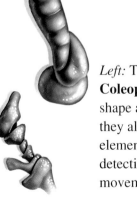

Left: The antennae of **Coleoptera** vary in shape and size, but they all have sensory elements capable of detecting smells or movements in the air.

EVERYTHING IS EDIBLE

The food habits of **Coleoptera** are very variable and sometimes the diets of the adult and the larvae are different. The mouth apparatus of the beetle is made up of several pieces: upper lip, mandibles, maxillae, lower lip, and **palps**. With their mandibles they grasp food, cut it and break it into small pieces.

Most beetles eat vegetable matter like fungi, fruit, wood, nectar, and pollen. The part of the plant that they prefer varies from one species to another. Some avidly devour the leaves of plants while others prefer the stalks and still others, the roots. The **xylophagous** species eat wood, excavating long tunnels inside trees, while some prefer shoots, fruit, or seeds.

One species of beetle eats feathers, clothes, and leather. **Necrophagous** beetles eat dead animals and **coprophagous** beetles eat excrement. There are few that are **parasites**, but some larvae develop inside beehives or wasp nests and eat their larvae.

Some are predators, and eat small insects, worms, and aphids. Some have a preference for one fixed type of prey, such as snails, while others live in ant or termite nests and feed their own larvae with these insects.

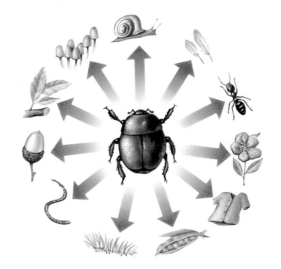

Right: A "snail-hunter" ground beetle eating a snail, which produces a secretion-like foam to defend itself. Another prefers a worm.

Left: Diagram of the food resources exploited by different types of beetles.

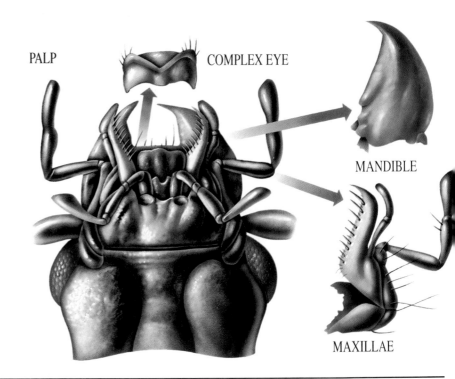

PALP

COMPLEX EYE

MANDIBLE

MAXILLAE

LOOKING FOR A MATE

At the start of the mating season beetles become very active. They have to find a mate. How do they recognize them? To locate and identify their partner some emit sounds. Some emit olfactory signals, and others, light.

Many females secrete substances called **pheromones** to attract males, who then detect the smell over large distances by means of their antennae.

At dusk, female glowworms, which have no wings and look like larvae, give out light (a luminous signal), through an organ located at the tip of the abdomen. The flashing attracts the male, which begins to circle around the female and finally comes to her side. The male can also emit luminous signals.

Sometimes male beetles oppose one another and fight for a female, although the duels are a ritual and the beetles do not usually cause any harm to each other.

During courtship, the male makes curious movements with its antennae to stimulate the female. Mating usually takes a very short time. The male places himself on top of the female and holds her with his legs.

Sometimes it is difficult at first sight to tell whether a beetle is male or female, but often the difference is obvious from the variations in shape, color, outline, and size. The males of some species have long horns on their heads, like the Hercules beetle. In some **Coleoptera** their **sexual dimorphism** is very marked. For instance the male stag beetle has enormous mandibles and is bigger than the female.

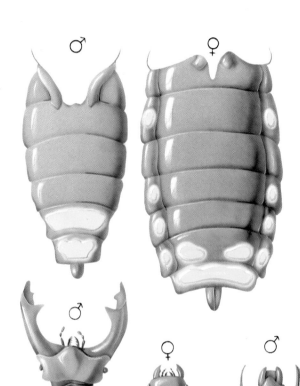

Above: Some females are wingless and their bodies resemble larvae, such as the glowworm, which cannot fly, but whose light attracts the male.

Left: Luminous organs in the abdomen of the male and female glowworm. *Below,* two examples of **sexual dimorphism**.

Right: Two male stag beetles fight for a female. On a branch, a pair of soldier beetles mating.

MOTHERS WITH FORESIGHT

In the course of their lives beetles go through four distinct stages. Egg, larva, **nymph**, adult, or **imago**. The duration of the cycle varies from one species to another. Normally the larva stage is the longest and can last for many years. In contrast, the adult usually lives a short time, varying between a few weeks and two years.

Once she has been fertilized, the mother carefully chooses a safe place to lay her eggs, which are usually oval. Their number varies greatly from one **Coleoptera** to another: 20, 100... up to several thousand. They are either laid grouped together, or one by one in separate chambers.

Normally they lay their eggs near a food source for the future larvae and sometimes even inside it. Some also prepare nests where, together with their eggs, they store food.

Some beetles protect the eggs inside a cocoon or they make special nests.

Ladybugs stick them to the back of leaves, on a plant infested with aphids, their favorite food. Others lay them underground, under a tree trunk, or inside fruit or seeds. Others lay them inside the **ootheca** or egg case of grasshoppers or inside ant nests.

A short time after being laid, the larvae are born, and break the outside of the egg with their powerful mandibles, helped by movement of their bodies. Some larvae have special spikes on their head or abdomen that help them do this.

Left: The ladybug lays its eggs on a plant that has aphids.

Below: Diagram of the life cycle of a ladybug with its four stages: egg, larva, **nymph**, and adult.

Far Left: The ground beetle lays its eggs underground.

Right: The cockchafer lays its eggs in small holes in the ground in fields.

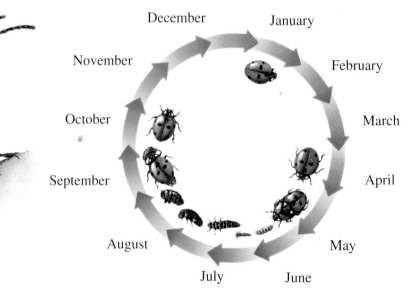

December · January · November · February · October · March · September · April · August · May · July · June

FROM LARVA TO NYMPH

Beetles, like butterflies and other insects, undergo changes before transforming themselves into adults. This is called **metamorphosis**. From the egg comes a small larva which does not resemble the adult at all. It has no wings or **elytra** and it is a very different shape.

Larvae usually have strong mandibles and various **ocelli** instead of complex eyes, and the majority have six legs, although some are **apodal**. Some are active, agile hunters and have long, strong legs. Scarab beetle larvae are soft and have a whitish body that is shaped like a C. They live underground and they eat roots. **Apodal** beetles look like maggots and they live inside their food source. Larvae eat a lot, and to grow they need to change their old skin for a newer, younger one, which is called moulting.

Beetles go through different stages of being a larva, often three. Usually they maintain the same appearance and habits throughout all three stages: they are **holometabolic**. However in some cases, each larval phase is different from the one before, both in appearance and in customs.

When its growth ends, the larva looks for a suitable place to transform itself into a **nymph**. Many bury themselves in the ground, while others hide themselves in hollows in trees, and some cling to leaves or branches. The **nymph** does not eat and

scarcely moves. During this phase of the cycle, major changes take place in its body: it grows **elytra** and wings and develops its eyes and more. Little by little the body transforms itself until it has turned into an adult, ending the **metamorphosis**.

Right: A male tiger beetle and a larva leaving its underground gallery lying in wait for a flightless wasp.

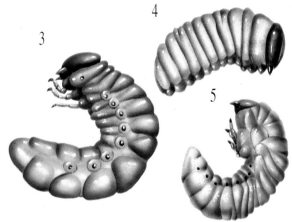

Above and left: Different types of larvae:
1. Leaf beetle.
2. Long-horned or wood-boring beetle.
3. Deathwatch beetle.
4. Weevil.
5. Cockchafer.

Below: Different larval phases during **metamorphosis**.

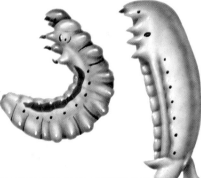

ARMS TO DEFEND ITSELF

Coleoptera have lots of enemies: Birds, some mammals, amphibians and reptiles, and even other insects or spiders can catch them.

To defend themselves from their enemies, beetles have recourse to some ingenious tricks. Most involve hiding and lying still until the danger has passed. Others pretend to be dead, and fall to the ground, absolutely motionless.

Some species, thanks to their ability to change color, camouflage themselves with their surroundings, and avoid detection. They have subtle colors and it is very difficult to see them if they do not move.

On the other hand, some beetles do not need to hide, because they secrete a terrible-tasting liquid. Their bright colors act as a warning.

There are some that are completely harmless, but that imitate the design and color of poisonous animals: they are **mimetic**. There is one species that has black and yellow stripes, so that it looks a lot like a wasp, and in this way it deceives predators which confuse it with a wasp and so do not attack it.

The bombardier beetle uses a very efficient defense system: When it feels threatened, it powerfully ejects a stream of repellant liquid, which puts a potential aggressor to flight.

Finally, other species, when they are molested or feel threatened, emit a chirping sound.

Above: The wasp beetle is seen on flowers in springtime and is easily confused with wasps.

Above: This gray or dark-brown covered beetle with white marks camouflages itself against its surroundings because it looks for food in rotten wood or dead branches.

Below: A mantis devouring a beetle that it has trapped between its sharp legs.

Right: Bombardier beetles spray their **predators**, mostly ants and toads, with a liquid that they produce in blisters on their skin.

TRASH COLLECTORS

There are beetles that feed on the excrement of animals like sheep, cows, and horses.

They are dark colored **Coleoptera**, usually black. Their forelegs are strong and hairy and often armed with spikes.

These curious beetles excavate tunnels underground and fill them with excrement, which acts to nourish their larvae. In some species, the male and the female cooperate in the excavations, whereas in others it is the female who does all the work.

There are different ways of building their nests. Beetles of the genus **Geotrupes** hollow out a tunnel underneath a pile of excrement, from which branch various galleries that they fill with **dung**.

Some **dung** beetles (*Copris*) prepare a long tunnel, normally beneath the excrement. Then they roll balls of **dung** into a pear shape, and place the egg inside it.

The scarab beetle builds a nest a certain distance from a heap of excrement, which acts as its food. After cutting off a piece of dung, it shapes it into a ball. With its hind legs, it rolls the ball along while it walks backward. When it reaches the place it has chosen for its nest, it buries the pear-shaped ball of dung, and places the egg at one end of it.

Above: How a female breaks off and forms a ball of **dung**.

Right: A pair of **dung** beetles convey a ball of dung.

Below: Different types of **dung** beetle nests.

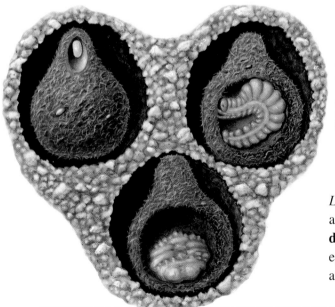

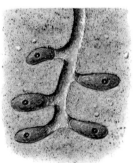

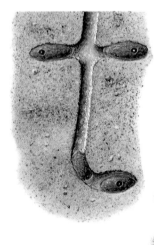

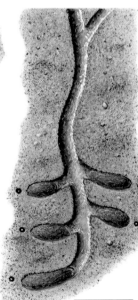

Left: Cross section of a pear-shaped ball of **dung**, containing an egg with the larva and chrysalis.

LEAF SCULPTORS

Some **Coleoptera** build amazing constructions. The female leaf-rolling weevil uses leaves of the trees where it lives, and with just its mandibles, constructs a very strange cover that it uses for a nest. These constructions serve to protect the eggs and the larvae, but they also guarantee them food.

When the time comes to lay her eggs, the female cuts the surface of a leaf on both sides of the central vein. Little by little the leaf rolls up within itself lengthwise, or from bottom to top, according to the species. In the first case the nest will be shaped like a cone or a cigar, whereas in the latter case it will be like a barrel. At first the nest-leaf will cling to the branch, but as it dries it will fall to the ground.

When the construction of the nest is complete, the female lays her eggs inside it. The young larvae that are born stay inside for a few weeks, until their development is over, feeding on the leaf that surrounds them. Then they leave their refuge and bury themselves in the ground, where they will spend the winter before transforming themselves into **nymphs**.

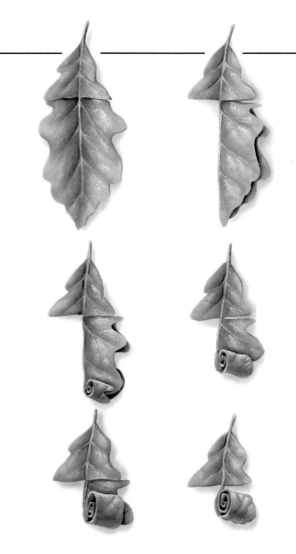

Right: A female leaf-rolling weevil constructing a nest with a birch leaf. This **Coleoptera** cuts, bends, and "binds" the leaves with a surprising skill.

Left and below: Sequence in the construction of a "cigar" made by a *Byctiscus populi* and a "barrel" made by an *Attelabus nitens*. The arrows show the direction of the fold.

SOME LIVE IN WATER

Aquatic beetles live in lakes, pools, and ponds, and even in rivers and streams.

Both the adult and the larva feed on small animals like insects, tadpoles, and young fish, although they will also eat dead fish if the opportunity presents itself.

The females lay their eggs among plants beneath the water. The larvae, like the adults, are aquatic, but the **nymph** phase takes place on dry land. The larva leaves the water and buries itself in a cell of clay that it constructs from the mud of the bank. Inside this cocoon it transforms itself into a nymph and then into the **imago**.

Diving beetles or *dytiscids* live beneath the water. Their hind legs are smooth with fine hairs, and they use them like oars, but for swimming. They rise to the surface to breathe, which they do by extending the tip of their abdomens out of the water, which is where their respiratory orifices are located.

Whirligig beetles are small aquatic beetles that stay on the surface of the water. Their eyes are divided into two parts, and in this way they can see under and out of the water at the same time. In case of danger, they submerge themselves. The larvae live under the water and do not need to leave it to breathe since they can take the oxygen that is dissolved in the water.

The larvae, which are elongated, have powerful mandibles with which they catch their prey. But they do not have a mouth. How do they eat? They inject a substance into the body of their prey, which dissolves its tissue and then they absorb it through channels inside their mandibles.

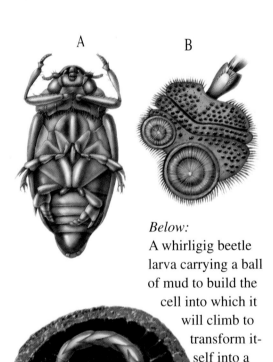

Above: A diving beetle larva extending the tip of its abdomen out of the water in order to breathe.

Left: A. Ventral view of an aquatic beetle, showing the adaptation of its rear limbs for swimming.

B. Male diving beetles have various suckers on their hind legs.

Right: At the bottom, an adult diving beetle and a larva that has caught a fish. On the surface a whirligig beetle and other diving beetles.

A   B

Below: A whirligig beetle larva carrying a ball of mud to build the cell into which it will climb to transform itself into a **nymph.**

DEVOURERS OF PLANTS

Many **Coleoptera**, both adults and larvae, can cause great damage to crops, woods, or food stores.

Many species feed on fruit, seeds, leaves, or roots, attacking all types of plants, including fruit trees, and vegetable crops.

The colorado or potato beetle, which originated in the United States, was accidentally introduced to Europe where it caused serious damage to crops. It is very voracious, and both adults and larvae feed on the leaves of that plant.

Some beetles destroy stored food (oats, wheat, maize, flour) and others attack fur, leather, and carpets causing great damage.

Many larvae and some adults feed on wood, weakening trees and causing damage in woods, fruit plantations, and parks. With their powerful mandibles, they dig out long tunnels from the wood. The infamous deathwatch beetle, which is frequently found in houses, destroys furniture, frames, beams and any other type of wood it finds in its path.

Bark beetles are **xylophagous Coleoptera** that attack different species of tree: birch, oak, elm, apple trees, pear trees, and cherry trees. They dig out central tunnels under the bark to lay their eggs. When they are born, the larvae open up side tunnels on either side of the central tunnel: They are **apodal** or legless, and chew away the wood tirelessly, lengthening and extending the tunnel as they grow.

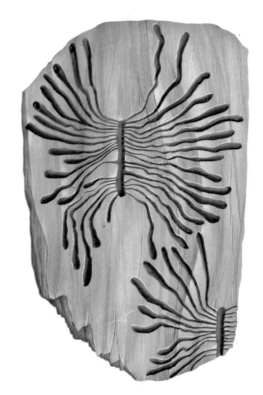

Right: Larvae and adults of the colorado or potato beetle.

Above: The death-watch beetle is a small, rarely seen beetle but it is unmistakeable for the holes that perforate any kind of wood, and for the little piles of dust it leaves in its path.

Left: The female bark beetle digs out a tunnel in the bark or in the wood and the larvae make their own tunnel.

Below: Grain weevils. The female lays her eggs inside the grains, so that the larvae can feed easily.

FRIENDS OF NATURE

We have seen that many beetles are harmful to humans. However there are some species that are extremely useful.

Beetles that feed on the nectar and pollen of flowers help plants to pollinate.

Some species are predators of harmful insects, and in this way they control their population and prevent them from becoming too numerous.

Others feed on the larvae of **xylophagous** insects, or hunt the caterpillars of butterflies that cause disease (such as pine caterpillars) or eat the larvae and adults of the potato beetle.

Nevertheless, the beetles that are most appreciated by humans are ladybugs. Many of these small **Coleoptera**, with their rounded, bright bodies, are excellent hunters of aphids, woodlice, acari, and fleas. For this reason ladybugs are used in the biological fight against the plague of these insects.

Necrophagous, or burying beetles, help nature because they aid the decomposition of dead animals. These **Coleoptera** have a well-developed sense of smell: they can detect a body by smell alone, often over great distances. The common carrion beetle excavates a tunnel beneath the dead animal, buries its body and then, with its powerful mandibles, breaks it up. The female lays its eggs beneath the ground, near the buried food so that when the larvae are born they will have food within easy reach. This female will care for the larvae in the early stages of their life, which is exceptional among these insects.

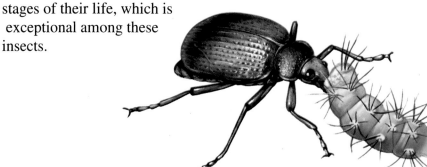

Right: An adult ladybug can eat up to a thousand aphids in a summer and can have up to a thousand offspring that will also be voracious eaters. Is there any better insecticide?

Left: **Necrophagous** or carrion beetles prefer bodies of small animals like rats, moles, and field mice.

Below: The ground beetle *Carabus granulatus* is a great exterminator of the potato beetle.

Above: A caterpillar hunter (*Calasoma*) devouring a caterpillar.

GLOSSARY

Apodal: An animal that has no feet.

Article: Each of the jointed pieces that form the legs.

Coleoptera: An insect that has a mouth for chewing, a solid shell, and two elytra that cover two membraneous wings.

Coprophage: An animal that eats excrement.

Decomposition: Transformation of a complex substance into something more simple.

Dung: Rotten, organic material, preferably of vegetable origin.

Elytrum: Each one of the two forewings of *Coleoptera,* which are hardened to protect the hindwings.

Holometabolous: An insect whose larvae are very different from the adult form.

Imago: Adult insect

Metamorphosis: Change that many animals undergo during their development.

Mimetic: The property some animals have of being the same coloring as other animals or objects in their environment.

Necrophagous: A *Coleoptera* that buries dead animals to feed its larvae.

Nymph: A young insect during metamorphosis.

Ocellus: Each simple eye that together form the complex eye of an insect.

Ommatidium: Complex eye.

Ootheca: Protective case that encloses the eggs of some insects

Palp: Each one of the jointed, mobile appendices that an insect has around its mouth to sense and control its food.

Parasite: An animal or vegetable that lives off of another, different species.

Pheromone: Chemical substance that some animals secrete and that affects the behavior of others.

Predator: An animal that hunts other animals for food.

Segment: Each one of the parts arranged in a line.

Sexual dimorphism: The condition in which the male and female of the same species take different forms.

Xylophagous: An insect that eats through wood.

INDEX